This House Hunting Journal Belongs To:

_____

ADDRESS *Information*

PREVIOUS ADDRESS:

REALTOR:
- NAME:
- AGENCY:
- PHONE:
- EMAIL:

CLOSING DATE:
DATE:

PREVIOUS ADDRESS:

REALTOR:
- NAME:
- AGENCY:
- PHONE:
- EMAIL:

CLOSING DATE:
DATE:

NOTES & REMINDERS

IMPORTANT *Contacts*

CLOSING ATTORNY

NAME:
ADDRESS:
EMAIL:
PHONE:

MORTGAGE BROKER / COMPANY

NAME:
ADDRESS:
EMAIL:
PHONE:

MOVING COMPANY

NAME:
ADDRESS:
EMAIL:
PHONE:

HOME APPRAISER

NAME:
ADDRESS:
EMAIL:
PHONE:

NOTES & REMINDERS

IMPORTANT *Contacts*

CLOSING ATTORNY

NAME:
ADDRESS:
EMAIL:
PHONE:

MORTGAGE BROKER / COMPANY

NAME:
ADDRESS:
EMAIL:
PHONE:

MOVING COMPANY

NAME:
ADDRESS:
EMAIL:
PHONE:

HOME APPRAISER

NAME:
ADDRESS:
EMAIL:
PHONE:

NOTES & REMINDERS

IMPORTANT *Dates*

MONTH:

NOTES & REMINDERS

PROPERTY INSPECTION *Checklist*

EXTERIOR CONDITION:
GOOD OK BAD **NOTES:**

- EXTERIOR OF PROPERTY
- FRONT DOOR
- PORCH/DECK/PATIO
- DRIVEWAY
- GARAGE DOORS
- OUTDOOR LIGHTING
- PAINT & TRIM
- WINDOWS
- WALKWAY

ROOF CONDITION:
GOOD OK BAD **NOTES:**

- CHIMNEY
- GUTTERS & DOWNSPOUTS
- SOFITS & FASCIA
- YEAR ROOF WAS REPLACED: _____

GARAGE CONDITION:
GOOD OK BAD **NOTES:**

- CEILING
- DOORS
- FLOORS & WALLS
- YEAR DOOR OPENERS WERE REPLACED: _____

YARD CONDITION:
GOOD OK BAD **NOTES:**

- DRAINAGE
- FENCES & GATES
- RETAINING WALL
- SPRINKLER SYSTEM

PROPERTY INSPECTION *Checklist*

OTHER IMPORTANT AREAS:	GOOD	OK	BAD	NOTES:
FOUNDATION				
MASONRY VENEERS				
EXTERIOR PAINT				
STORM WINDOWS				
PLUMBING				
ELECTRICAL OUTLETS				
FLOORING IN ROOMS				
WOOD TRIM				
FIREPLACE				

KITCHEN CONDITION:	GOOD	OK	BAD	NOTES:
WORKING EXHAUST FAN				
NO LEAKS IN PIPES				
APPLIANCES OPERATE				
OTHER:				

BATHROOM CONDITION:	GOOD	OK	BAD	NOTES:
PROPER DRAINAGE				
NO LEAKS IN PIPES				
CAULKING IN GOOD SHAPE				
TILES ARE SECURE				

MISC:	GOOD	OK	BAD	NOTES:
SMOKE & CARBON DETECTORS				
STAIRWAY TREADS SOLID				
STAIR HANDRAILS INSTALLED				
OTHER:				
OTHER:				
OTHER:				

HOUSE HUNTING *List*

ADDRESS	PRICE	NOTES

HOUSE HUNTING *List*

ADDRESS	PRICE	NOTES

HOUSE HUNTING *List*

ADDRESS	PRICE	NOTES

HOUSE HUNTING *List*

ADDRESS	PRICE	NOTES

HOUSE HUNTING *List*

ADDRESS	PRICE	NOTES

HOUSE HUNTING *List*

ADDRESS	PRICE	NOTES

HOUSE HUNTING *Checklist*

HOUSE SCORE:

PROPERTY ADDRESS

ASKING PRICE: PROPERTY TAXES:

LOT SIZE: PROPERTY SIZE:

FINISH: ☐ BRICK ☐ STUCCO ☐ WOOD ☐ SIDING AGE OF PROPERTY:

NEIGHBORHOOD

DISTANCE TO SCHOOLS: DISTANCE TO WORK:

PUBLIC TRANSPORTATION: MEDICAL:

RECREATION: SHOPPING:

ADDITIONAL INFO:

NOTES:

HOUSE HUNTING

DETAILED HOUSE FEATURES:

OF BEDROOMS: # OF BATHROOMS:

BASEMENT: HEATING TYPE:

PROPERTY CHECKLIST:

				NOTES
POOL	☐	BONUS ROOM	☐	
GARAGE	☐	LAUNDRY CHUTE	☐	
FIREPLACE	☐	FENCED YARD	☐	
EN-SUITE	☐	APPLIANCES	☐	
OFFICE	☐	A/C	☐	
DECK	☐	HEAT PUMP	☐	

NOTES

PARKING	☐
CLOSETS	☐
STORAGE	☐

HOUSE HUNTING
Checklist

HOUSE SCORE:

PROPERTY ADDRESS

ASKING PRICE: **PROPERTY TAXES:**

LOT SIZE: **PROPERTY SIZE:**

FINISH: ☐ BRICK ☐ STUCCO   **AGE OF PROPERTY:**
☐ WOOD ☐ SIDING

NEIGHBORHOOD

DISTANCE TO SCHOOLS: **DISTANCE TO WORK:**

PUBLIC TRANSPORTATION: **MEDICAL:**

RECREATION: **SHOPPING:**

ADDITIONAL INFO: **NOTES:**

HOUSE HUNTING

DETAILED HOUSE FEATURES:

OF BEDROOMS: # OF BATHROOMS:

BASEMENT: HEATING TYPE:

PROPERTY CHECKLIST:

				NOTES
POOL	☐	BONUS ROOM	☐	
GARAGE	☐	LAUNDRY CHUTE	☐	
FIREPLACE	☐	FENCED YARD	☐	
EN-SUITE	☐	APPLIANCES	☐	
OFFICE	☐	A/C	☐	
DECK	☐	HEAT PUMP	☐	

		NOTES
PARKING	☐	
CLOSETS	☐	
STORAGE	☐	

HOUSE HUNTING
Checklist

HOUSE SCORE:

PROPERTY ADDRESS

ASKING PRICE: PROPERTY TAXES:

LOT SIZE: PROPERTY SIZE:

FINISH: ☐ BRICK ☐ STUCCO   AGE OF PROPERTY:
        ☐ WOOD   ☐ SIDING

NEIGHBORHOOD

DISTANCE TO SCHOOLS: DISTANCE TO WORK:

PUBLIC TRANSPORTATION: MEDICAL:

RECREATION: SHOPPING:

ADDITIONAL INFO: NOTES:

HOUSE HUNTING

DETAILED HOUSE FEATURES:

OF BEDROOMS: # OF BATHROOMS:

BASEMENT: HEATING TYPE:

PROPERTY CHECKLIST:

			NOTES
POOL ☐	BONUS ROOM ☐		
GARAGE ☐	LAUNDRY CHUTE ☐		
FIREPLACE ☐	FENCED YARD ☐		
EN-SUITE ☐	APPLIANCES ☐		
OFFICE ☐	A/C ☐		
DECK ☐	HEAT PUMP ☐		

NOTES

- PARKING ☐
- CLOSETS ☐
- STORAGE ☐

☐
☐
☐
☐
☐
☐
☐
☐
☐

HOUSE HUNTING
Checklist

HOUSE SCORE:

PROPERTY ADDRESS

ASKING PRICE: PROPERTY TAXES:

LOT SIZE: PROPERTY SIZE:

FINISH: ☐ BRICK   ☐ STUCCO   AGE OF PROPERTY:
          ☐ WOOD   ☐ SIDING

NEIGHBORHOOD

DISTANCE TO SCHOOLS: DISTANCE TO WORK:

PUBLIC TRANSPORTATION: MEDICAL:

RECREATION: SHOPPING:

ADDITIONAL INFO: NOTES:

HOUSE HUNTING

DETAILED HOUSE FEATURES:

OF BEDROOMS: # OF BATHROOMS:

BASEMENT: HEATING TYPE:

PROPERTY CHECKLIST:

		NOTES
POOL ☐	BONUS ROOM ☐	
GARAGE ☐	LAUNDRY CHUTE ☐	
FIREPLACE ☐	FENCED YARD ☐	
EN-SUITE ☐	APPLIANCES ☐	
OFFICE ☐	A/C ☐	
DECK ☐	HEAT PUMP ☐	

	NOTES
PARKING ☐	
CLOSETS ☐	
STORAGE ☐	

HOUSE HUNTING Checklist

HOUSE SCORE:

PROPERTY ADDRESS

ASKING PRICE: **PROPERTY TAXES:**

LOT SIZE: **PROPERTY SIZE:**

FINISH: ☐ BRICK ☐ STUCCO ☐ WOOD ☐ SIDING **AGE OF PROPERTY:**

NEIGHBORHOOD

DISTANCE TO SCHOOLS: **DISTANCE TO WORK:**

PUBLIC TRANSPORTATION: **MEDICAL:**

RECREATION: **SHOPPING:**

ADDITIONAL INFO:

NOTES:

HOUSE HUNTING

DETAILED HOUSE FEATURES:

OF BEDROOMS: # OF BATHROOMS:

BASEMENT: HEATING TYPE:

PROPERTY CHECKLIST:

				NOTES
POOL	☐	BONUS ROOM	☐	
GARAGE	☐	LAUNDRY CHUTE	☐	
FIREPLACE	☐	FENCED YARD	☐	
EN-SUITE	☐	APPLIANCES	☐	
OFFICE	☐	A/C	☐	
DECK	☐	HEAT PUMP	☐	

		NOTES
PARKING	☐	
CLOSETS	☐	
STORAGE	☐	

HOUSE HUNTING *Checklist*

HOUSE SCORE:

PROPERTY ADDRESS

ASKING PRICE:

PROPERTY TAXES:

LOT SIZE:

PROPERTY SIZE:

FINISH:
- ☐ BRICK
- ☐ STUCCO
- ☐ WOOD
- ☐ SIDING

AGE OF PROPERTY:

NEIGHBORHOOD

DISTANCE TO SCHOOLS:

DISTANCE TO WORK:

PUBLIC TRANSPORTATION:

MEDICAL:

RECREATION:

SHOPPING:

ADDITIONAL INFO:

NOTES:

HOUSE HUNTING

DETAILED HOUSE FEATURES:

OF BEDROOMS: # OF BATHROOMS:

BASEMENT: HEATING TYPE:

PROPERTY CHECKLIST:

				NOTES
POOL	☐	BONUS ROOM	☐	
GARAGE	☐	LAUNDRY CHUTE	☐	
FIREPLACE	☐	FENCED YARD	☐	
EN-SUITE	☐	APPLIANCES	☐	
OFFICE	☐	A/C	☐	
DECK	☐	HEAT PUMP	☐	

		NOTES
PARKING	☐	
CLOSETS	☐	
STORAGE	☐	
	☐	
	☐	
	☐	
	☐	
	☐	
	☐	
	☐	

HOUSE HUNTING

HOUSE SCORE:

PROPERTY ADDRESS

ASKING PRICE: PROPERTY TAXES:

LOT SIZE: PROPERTY SIZE:

FINISH: ☐ BRICK ☐ STUCCO   AGE OF PROPERTY:
         ☐ WOOD   ☐ SIDING

NEIGHBORHOOD

DISTANCE TO SCHOOLS: DISTANCE TO WORK:

PUBLIC TRANSPORTATION: MEDICAL:

RECREATION: SHOPPING:

ADDITIONAL INFO: NOTES:

HOUSE HUNTING

DETAILED HOUSE FEATURES:

OF BEDROOMS: # OF BATHROOMS:

BASEMENT: HEATING TYPE:

PROPERTY CHECKLIST:

				NOTES
POOL	☐	BONUS ROOM	☐	
GARAGE	☐	LAUNDRY CHUTE	☐	
FIREPLACE	☐	FENCED YARD	☐	
EN-SUITE	☐	APPLIANCES	☐	
OFFICE	☐	A/C	☐	
DECK	☐	HEAT PUMP	☐	

		NOTES
PARKING	☐	
CLOSETS	☐	
STORAGE	☐	

House Hunting NOTES

House Hunting NOTES

House Hunting *NOTES*

House Hunting *NOTES*

House Hunting NOTES

House Hunting *NOTES*

House Hunting NOTES

BUDGET & *Expenses*

PREVIOUS RESIDENCE

EXPENSES	BUDGET	ACTUAL	DIFFERENCE

NEW RESIDENCE

EXPENSES	BUDGET	ACTUAL	DIFFERENCE

OTHER

EXPENSES	BUDGET	ACTUAL	DIFFERENCE

TO DO: *Previous Residence*

DATE:

MOST IMPORTANT

NOTES:

TO DO: *New Residence*

DATE:

MOST IMPORTANT

NOTES:

MOVING DAY *Planner*

PRIORITIES

MOVING DAY SCHEDULE

6 AM
7 AM
8 AM
9 AM
10 AM
11 AM
12 PM
1 PM
2 PM
3 PM
4 PM
5 PM
6 PM
7 PM
8 PM
9 PM
10 PM
11 PM
12 AM

MOVING DAY TO DO LIST

ORGANIZATION

REMINDERS

MOVING DAY *List*

OLD RESIDENCE

NEW RESIDENCE

MOVING DAY *List*

OLD RESIDENCE	NEW RESIDENCE

Packing NOTES

Packing NOTES

Packing NOTES

Packing NOTES

ADDRESS CHANGE Checklist

UTILITIES:

- ELECTRIC
- CABLE/SATELLITE
- GAS
- SECURITY SYSTEM
- PHONE
- INTERNET
- WATER/SEWER
- OTHER
- OTHER
- OTHER

FINANCIAL:

- BANK
- CREDIT CARD
- BANK STATEMENTS
- EMPLOYER
- INSURANCE
- OTHER
- OTHER
- OTHER
- OTHER
- OTHER

START/STOP *Utilities*

ELECTRIC COMPANY

- **NAME**
- **PHONE**
- **WEBSITE URL**
- **START DATE**
- **STOP DATE**
- **ACCOUNT NUMBER**

CABLE / SATELLITE

- **NAME**
- **PHONE**
- **WEBSITE URL**
- **START DATE**
- **STOP DATE**
- **ACCOUNT NUMBER**

GAS / HEATING COMPANY

- **NAME**
- **PHONE**
- **WEBSITE URL**
- **START DATE**
- **STOP DATE**
- **ACCOUNT NUMBER**

START/STOP *Utilities*

INTERNET PROVIDER

NAME

PHONE

WEBSITE URL

START DATE

STOP DATE

ACCOUNT NUMBER

SECURITY SYSTEM

NAME

PHONE

WEBSITE URL

START DATE

STOP DATE

ACCOUNT NUMBER

OTHER:

NAME

PHONE

WEBSITE URL

START DATE

STOP DATE

ACCOUNT NUMBER

NOTES:

NEW PROVIDER *Contacts*

MEDICAL

FAMILY DOCTOR

NAME:
PHONE:
EMAIL:
ADDRESS:
WEBSITE URL:

DENTIST

NAME:
PHONE:
EMAIL:
ADDRESS:
WEBSITE URL:

PEDIATRICIAN

NAME:
PHONE:
EMAIL:
ADDRESS:
WEBSITE URL:

NOTES

NEW PROVIDER *Contacts*

EDUCATION

SCHOOL #1:

NAME:
PHONE:
EMAIL:
ADDRESS:
WEBSITE URL:

SCHOOL #2:

NAME:
PHONE:
EMAIL:
ADDRESS:
WEBSITE URL:

SCHOOL #3:

NAME:
PHONE:
EMAIL:
ADDRESS:
WEBSITE URL:

NOTES

MOVING DAY *Planner*

6-WEEKS PRIOR

- [ ] HIRE A MOVING COMPANY
- [ ] KEEP RECEIPTS FOR TAX PURPOSES
- [ ] DETERMINE A BUDGET FOR MOVING EXPENSES
- [ ] ORGANIZE INVENTORY
- [ ] GET PACKING BOXES & LABELS
- [ ] PURGE / GIVE AWAY / SELL UNWANTED ITEMS
- [ ] CREATE AN INVENTORY SHEET OF ITEMS & BOXES
- [ ] RESEARCH SCHOOLS FOR YOUR CHILDREN
- [ ] PLAN A GARAGE SALE TO UNLOAD UNWANTED ITEMS

4-WEEKS PRIOR

- [ ] CONFIRM DATES WITH MOVING COMPANY
- [ ] RESEARCH YOUR NEW COMMUNITY
- [ ] START PACKING BOXES
- [ ] PURCHASE MOVING INSURANCE
- [ ] ORGANIZE FINANCIAL & LEGAL DOCUMENTS IN ONE PLACE
- [ ] FIND SNOW REMOVAL OR LANDSCAPE SERVICE FOR NEW RESIDENCE
- [ ] RESEARCH NEW DOCTOR, DENTIST, VETERNARIAN, ETC

2-WEEKS PRIOR

- [ ] PLAN FOR PET TRANSPORT DURING MOVE
- [ ] SET UP MAIL FORWARDING SERVICE
- [ ] TRANSFER HOMEOWNERS INSURANCE TO NEW RESIDENCE
- [ ] TRANSFER UTILITIES TO NEW RESIDENCE
- [ ] UPDATE YOUR DRIVER'S LICENSE

MOVING DAY *Planner*

6-WEEKS PRIOR

4-WEEKS PRIOR

2-WEEKS PRIOR

MOVING DAY *Planner*

WEEK OF MOVE

MOVING DAY

NOTES & REMINDERS

IMPORTANT DATES

Month

Notes

MOVING BOX *Inventory*

ROOM: **BOX NO:**   **COLOR CODE:**

CONTENTS:

ROOM: **BOX NO:**   **COLOR CODE:**

CONTENTS:

ROOM: **BOX NO:**   **COLOR CODE:**

CONTENTS:

ROOM: **BOX NO:**   **COLOR CODE:**

CONTENTS:

MOVING BOX *Inventory*

ROOM: **BOX NO:**   **COLOR CODE:**

CONTENTS:

ROOM: **BOX NO:**   **COLOR CODE:**

CONTENTS:

ROOM: **BOX NO:**   **COLOR CODE:**

CONTENTS:

ROOM: **BOX NO:**   **COLOR CODE:**

CONTENTS:

MOVING BOX *Inventory*

ROOM: BOX NO: COLOR CODE:

CONTENTS:

ROOM: BOX NO: COLOR CODE:

CONTENTS:

ROOM: BOX NO: COLOR CODE:

CONTENTS:

ROOM: BOX NO: COLOR CODE:

CONTENTS:

MOVING BOX *Inventory*

ROOM: BOX NO: COLOR CODE:

CONTENTS:

ROOM: BOX NO: COLOR CODE:

CONTENTS:

ROOM: BOX NO: COLOR CODE:

CONTENTS:

ROOM: BOX NO: COLOR CODE:

CONTENTS:

MOVING BOX *Inventory*

ROOM: BOX NO: COLOR CODE:

CONTENTS:

ROOM: BOX NO: COLOR CODE:

CONTENTS:

ROOM: BOX NO: COLOR CODE:

CONTENTS:

ROOM: BOX NO: COLOR CODE:

CONTENTS:

MOVING BOX *Inventory*

ROOM: BOX NO: COLOR CODE:

CONTENTS:

ROOM: BOX NO: COLOR CODE:

CONTENTS:

ROOM: BOX NO: COLOR CODE:

CONTENTS:

ROOM: BOX NO: COLOR CODE:

CONTENTS:

MOVING BOX *Inventory*

ROOM: **BOX NO:**   **COLOR CODE:**

CONTENTS:

ROOM: **BOX NO:**   **COLOR CODE:**

CONTENTS:

ROOM: **BOX NO:**   **COLOR CODE:**

CONTENTS:

ROOM: **BOX NO:**   **COLOR CODE:**

CONTENTS:

MOVING BOX *Inventory*

ROOM: **BOX NO:**   **COLOR CODE:**

CONTENTS:

ROOM: **BOX NO:**   **COLOR CODE:**

CONTENTS:

ROOM: **BOX NO:**   **COLOR CODE:**

CONTENTS:

ROOM: **BOX NO:**   **COLOR CODE:**

CONTENTS:

MOVING BOX *Inventory*

ROOM:	BOX NO:	COLOR CODE:
CONTENTS:		

ROOM:	BOX NO:	COLOR CODE:
CONTENTS:		

ROOM:	BOX NO:	COLOR CODE:
CONTENTS:		

ROOM:	BOX NO:	COLOR CODE:
CONTENTS:		

MOVING BOX *Inventory*

ROOM: BOX NO: COLOR CODE:

CONTENTS:

ROOM: BOX NO: COLOR CODE:

CONTENTS:

ROOM: BOX NO: COLOR CODE:

CONTENTS:

ROOM: BOX NO: COLOR CODE:

CONTENTS:

MOVING BOX *Inventory*

ROOM:	BOX NO:	COLOR CODE:

CONTENTS:

ROOM:	BOX NO:	COLOR CODE:

CONTENTS:

ROOM:	BOX NO:	COLOR CODE:

CONTENTS:

ROOM:	BOX NO:	COLOR CODE:

CONTENTS:

MOVING BOX *Inventory*

ROOM: BOX NO: COLOR CODE:

CONTENTS:

ROOM: BOX NO: COLOR CODE:

CONTENTS:

ROOM: BOX NO: COLOR CODE:

CONTENTS:

ROOM: BOX NO: COLOR CODE:

CONTENTS:

MOVING BOX *Inventory*

ROOM: **BOX NO:** **COLOR CODE:**

CONTENTS:

ROOM: **BOX NO:** **COLOR CODE:**

CONTENTS:

ROOM: **BOX NO:** **COLOR CODE:**

CONTENTS:

ROOM: **BOX NO:** **COLOR CODE:**

CONTENTS:

MOVING BOX *Inventory*

ROOM: **BOX NO:**   **COLOR CODE:**

CONTENTS:

ROOM: **BOX NO:**   **COLOR CODE:**

CONTENTS:

ROOM: **BOX NO:**   **COLOR CODE:**

CONTENTS:

ROOM: **BOX NO:**   **COLOR CODE:**

CONTENTS:

MOVING BOX *Inventory*

ROOM: BOX NO: COLOR CODE:

CONTENTS:

ROOM: BOX NO: COLOR CODE:

CONTENTS:

ROOM: BOX NO: COLOR CODE:

CONTENTS:

ROOM: BOX NO: COLOR CODE:

CONTENTS:

MOVING BOX *Inventory*

ROOM: BOX NO: COLOR CODE:

CONTENTS:

ROOM: BOX NO: COLOR CODE:

CONTENTS:

ROOM: BOX NO: COLOR CODE:

CONTENTS:

ROOM: BOX NO: COLOR CODE:

CONTENTS:

MOVING BOX *Inventory*

ROOM: **BOX NO:**   **COLOR CODE:**

CONTENTS:

ROOM: **BOX NO:**   **COLOR CODE:**

CONTENTS:

ROOM: **BOX NO:**   **COLOR CODE:**

CONTENTS:

ROOM: **BOX NO:**   **COLOR CODE:**

CONTENTS:

MOVING BOX *Inventory*

ROOM: **BOX NO:**   **COLOR CODE:**

CONTENTS:

ROOM: **BOX NO:**   **COLOR CODE:**

CONTENTS:

ROOM: **BOX NO:**   **COLOR CODE:**

CONTENTS:

ROOM: **BOX NO:**   **COLOR CODE:**

CONTENTS:

MOVING BOX *Inventory*

ROOM: **BOX NO:**   **COLOR CODE:**

CONTENTS:

ROOM: **BOX NO:**   **COLOR CODE:**

CONTENTS:

ROOM: **BOX NO:**   **COLOR CODE:**

CONTENTS:

ROOM: **BOX NO:**   **COLOR CODE:**

CONTENTS:

MOVING BOX *Inventory*

ROOM: **BOX NO:**   **COLOR CODE:**

CONTENTS:

ROOM: **BOX NO:**   **COLOR CODE:**

CONTENTS:

ROOM: **BOX NO:**   **COLOR CODE:**

CONTENTS:

ROOM: **BOX NO:**   **COLOR CODE:**

CONTENTS:

MOVING BOX *Inventory*

ROOM:	BOX NO:	COLOR CODE:

CONTENTS:

ROOM:	BOX NO:	COLOR CODE:

CONTENTS:

ROOM:	BOX NO:	COLOR CODE:

CONTENTS:

ROOM:	BOX NO:	COLOR CODE:

CONTENTS:

MOVING BOX *Inventory*

ROOM: **BOX NO:**   **COLOR CODE:**

CONTENTS:

ROOM: **BOX NO:**   **COLOR CODE:**

CONTENTS:

ROOM: **BOX NO:**   **COLOR CODE:**

CONTENTS:

ROOM: **BOX NO:**   **COLOR CODE:**

CONTENTS:

MOVING BOX *Inventory*

ROOM: **BOX NO:**   **COLOR CODE:**

CONTENTS:

ROOM: **BOX NO:**   **COLOR CODE:**

CONTENTS:

ROOM: **BOX NO:**   **COLOR CODE:**

CONTENTS:

ROOM: **BOX NO:**   **COLOR CODE:**

CONTENTS:

MOVING BOX *Inventory*

ROOM: BOX NO: COLOR CODE:

CONTENTS:

ROOM: BOX NO: COLOR CODE:

CONTENTS:

ROOM: BOX NO: COLOR CODE:

CONTENTS:

ROOM: BOX NO: COLOR CODE:

CONTENTS:

MOVING BOX *Inventory*

ROOM: **BOX NO:**   **COLOR CODE:**

CONTENTS:

ROOM: **BOX NO:**   **COLOR CODE:**

CONTENTS:

ROOM: **BOX NO:**   **COLOR CODE:**

CONTENTS:

ROOM: **BOX NO:**   **COLOR CODE:**

CONTENTS:

ROOM *Planner*

ROOM:

PAINT COLORS::

COLOR SCHEME:

DÉCOR IDEAS:

FURNITURE IDEAS:

NOTES:

ROOM:

PAINT COLORS::

COLOR SCHEME:

DÉCOR IDEAS:

FURNITURE IDEAS:

NOTES:

NEW ROOM *Planner*

ROOM:

PAINT COLORS::

COLOR CODE:

DÉCOR IDEAS:

FURNITURE IDEAS:

THINGS TO DO:

☐
☐
☐
☐
☐
☐
☐
☐
☐
☐
☐

DÉCOR IDEAS:

ROOM *Planner*

ROOM:

PAINT COLORS::

COLOR SCHEME:

DÉCOR IDEAS:

FURNITURE IDEAS:

NOTES:

ROOM:

PAINT COLORS::

COLOR SCHEME:

DÉCOR IDEAS:

FURNITURE IDEAS:

NOTES:

NEW ROOM *Planner*

ROOM:

PAINT COLORS::

COLOR CODE:

DÉCOR IDEAS:

FURNITURE IDEAS:

THINGS TO DO:

- [ ]
- [ ]
- [ ]
- [ ]
- [ ]
- [ ]
- [ ]
- [ ]
- [ ]
- [ ]
- [ ]

DÉCOR IDEAS:

ROOM *Planner*

ROOM:

PAINT COLORS::

COLOR SCHEME:

DÉCOR IDEAS:

FURNITURE IDEAS:

NOTES:

ROOM:

PAINT COLORS::

COLOR SCHEME:

DÉCOR IDEAS:

FURNITURE IDEAS:

NOTES:

NEW ROOM *Planner*

ROOM:

PAINT COLORS::

COLOR CODE:

DÉCOR IDEAS:

FURNITURE IDEAS:

THINGS TO DO:

- ☐
- ☐
- ☐
- ☐
- ☐
- ☐
- ☐
- ☐
- ☐
- ☐
- ☐

DÉCOR IDEAS:

ROOM *Planner*

ROOM:

PAINT COLORS::

COLOR SCHEME:

DÉCOR IDEAS:

FURNITURE IDEAS:

NOTES:

ROOM:

PAINT COLORS::

COLOR SCHEME:

DÉCOR IDEAS:

FURNITURE IDEAS:

NOTES:

NEW ROOM *Planner*

ROOM:

PAINT COLORS::

COLOR CODE:

DÉCOR IDEAS:

FURNITURE IDEAS:

THINGS TO DO:

- [ ]
- [ ]
- [ ]
- [ ]
- [ ]
- [ ]
- [ ]
- [ ]
- [ ]
- [ ]
- [ ]

DÉCOR IDEAS:

ROOM *Planner*

ROOM:

PAINT COLORS::

COLOR SCHEME:

DÉCOR IDEAS:

FURNITURE IDEAS:

NOTES:

ROOM:

PAINT COLORS::

COLOR SCHEME:

DÉCOR IDEAS:

FURNITURE IDEAS:

NOTES:

NEW ROOM *Planner*

ROOM:

PAINT COLORS::

COLOR CODE:

DÉCOR IDEAS:

FURNITURE IDEAS:

THINGS TO DO:

- [ ]
- [ ]
- [ ]
- [ ]
- [ ]
- [ ]
- [ ]
- [ ]
- [ ]
- [ ]
- [ ]

DÉCOR IDEAS:

My Personal NOTES

My Personal NOTES

My Personal NOTES

My Personal NOTES

My Personal NOTES

My Personal NOTES

My Personal NOTES

My Personal NOTES

My Personal NOTES

My Personal NOTES

My Personal NOTES

My Personal NOTES

www.ingramcontent.com/pod-product-compliance
Lightning Source LLC
Chambersburg PA
CBHW022109170526
45157CB00004B/1550